My First Grade

Koine Greek reader

Αναγνώστης της πρώτης μου τάξης

Thomas Moore

AuthorHouse™
1663 Liberty Drive
Bloomington, IN 47403
www.authorhouse.com
Phone: 833-262-8899

Because of the dynamic nature of the Internet, any web addresses or links contained in this book may have changed
since publication and may no longer be valid. The views expressed in this work are solely those of the author and do
not necessarily reflect the views of the publisher, and the publisher hereby disclaims any responsibility for them.

Any people depicted in stock imagery provided by Getty Images are models,
and such images are being used for illustrative purposes only.
Certain stock imagery © Getty Images.

This book is printed on acid-free paper.

The Greek New Testament text was published in 1904: Public Domain.

Graphic Images were all created by Microsoft Bing Copilot Pro.

ISBN: 979-8-8230-3189-9 (sc)
ISBN: 979-8-8230-3193-6 (hc)
ISBN: 979-8-8230-3192-9 (e)

Library of Congress Control Number: 2024916925

Print information available on the last page.

Published by AuthorHouse 08/28/2024

authorHOUSE®

ἀναγνωστικόν (anagnostikon): This is a neuter singular noun in the nominative case, derived from the verb "ἀναγιγνώσκω" (anagignosko), meaning "to read." It refers to a "reader," which is a book or collection of texts used for learning to read.

μου (mou): This is the first person singular possessive pronoun "my." It shows ownership or association with the speaker.

τῆς (tēs): This is the feminine singular genitive case of the definite article "the." It is used here to denote possession, as in "of the."

πρώτης (prōtēs): This is an adjective in the feminine singular genitive case, meaning "first." It qualifies the noun "τάξεως" (taxeos), indicating the first grade or level.

τάξεως (taxeos): This is a feminine singular noun in the genitive case, meaning "grade" or "class." It refers to the level of schooling or education.

So, the phrase written in Greek translates to "The reader of mine of the first grade."

John 6:35

Εἶπεν (Eipen) - Said **αὐτοῖς (autois)** - to them **ὁ (ho)** - the **Ἰησοῦς (Iēsous)** - Jesus **Ἐγώ (Egō)** - I

εἰμι (eimi) - am **ὁ (ho)** - the **ἄρτος (artos)** - bread **τῆς (tēs)** - of the **ζωῆς (zōēs)** - life **ὁ (ho)** - the [one]

ἐρχόμενος (erchomenos) - coming **πρὸς (pros)** - to **ἐμὲ (eme)** - Me **οὐ (ou)** - never **μὴ (mē)** - not

πεινάσῃ (peinasē) - shall hunger **καὶ (kai)** - and **ὁ (ho)** - the [one] **πιστεύων (pisteuōn)** - believing

εἰς (eis) - in **ἐμὲ (eme)** - Me **οὐ (ou)** - no **μὴ (mē)** - not **διψήσει (dipsēsei)** - shall thirst **πώποτε (pōpote)** - at any time

Preface

For those who are students of the Koine Greek, I offer this book as an enjoyable way to grow in understanding and familiarity with Biblical Greek as simple Greek verses have been collected to provide encouragement and inspiration for those seeking expertise in the Koine Greek.

To me, there is nothing more enjoyable than being able to sit down in a comfy chair and read the Scriptures in the actual language of the Apostles. When I first memorized Revelations 4:8 in the Greek, I went outside after midnight, looked up at the stars and was so elated to say aloud:

ἅγιος, ἅγιος, ἅγιος Κύριος ὁ Θεὸς ὁ παντοκράτωρ, ὁ ἦν καὶ ὁ ὢν καὶ ὁ ἐρχόμενος.

It was such a joy to worship the Lord Jesus in the actual language in which this verse was originally written and spoken all over the entire Hellenistic world. It is such a wonderful experience that I want to share this joy with my brothers and sisters in Christ. The way that I learned these verses was by creating a first-grade reader for myself. Then as I mastered the first-grade reader, I created a second-grade reader and now have made for myself a third-grade reader.

I got tired of Greek textbooks that focus on grammar, instead of just enjoying the language. When do I get to just sit down and enjoy reading simple sentences in Greek to get familiar with the language? When I was a child, I learned English and was able to communicate clearly in English without knowing anything about a predicate nominatives, pluperfect, or adverbs. Why can't I learn Greek the same way I learned English. I was only introduced to predicate nominatives when I attained the sixth grade. How about we don't discuss predicate nominatives until I am reading Greek at the sixth-grade level. The way the Greek language is taught, is assuming a person has a full grasp of English grammar. Some people love grammar, and they can absorb it like a sponge. I am not that way. I did not get decent grades in grammar and find it hard to memorize all those rules. Most five-year-olds can read and speak proficiently, but don't know grammar.

What I look forward to is being able to read the language in a collection of verses that target my reading proficiency level, which I find to be an exceedingly wonderful experience. Myself, I am working hard to attain to the proficiency that William Mounce calls "baby Greek," but until then, I love sitting in my favorite chair each morning with a cup of coffee and then submerge myself into the beautiful Koine Greek Scriptures that match my abilities. In this process I am learning the flow of the language, and becoming familiar with how Greek words morph into different words or add meaning with prefix morphs, which are all essential to learn, since they are so foreign to English.

If a person has acquired this book, who has never studied Greek at all, then I suggest they use the fantastic learning tools that I used and purchase these books:

Basic Greek in 30 Minutes a Day by James Found. My first Koine Greek workbook: FANTASTIC!

English-Greek Reverse Interlinear New Testament in *ESV* by Crossway Books or…

Interlinear for the Rest of Us (includes a Greek English dictionary) by William Mounce.

Greek for the Rest of Us by William Mounce, plus get the Laminated sheet!

A huge help is purchase the entire Greek bundle: _Learn Biblical Greek Pack 2.0_: Includes _Basics of Biblical Greek Grammar_, Fourth Edition and Its Supporting Resources by William D. Mounce. It has everything you could ever want including verbal audio pronunciation and video lectures. AWESOME!

My thanks to William Mounce: a treasure to the Body of Christ for helping us all learn Greek. My thanks also to James Found, author of my very first Greek Workbook.

When you become familiar with the Koine Greek, then you can embark on very rewarding word studies that you find in book sets like: *Robertson's Word Pictures* and *Gerhard Kittle's Theological Dictionary of the New Testament*, either in the single volume Bromiley put together or the one I enjoy is the full 10 volume set of *Kittle's Theological Dictionary of the New Testament*. A book I refer to often is *Mounce's Complete Expository Dictionary of Old and New Testament Words* by William D. Mounce. Also helpful is: *Dictionary of New Testament Theology* by Colin Brown (three volumes).

Being familiar with the Greek you will be able to enjoy the brilliant insights into Scripture that you find in *Meyer's Exegetical Handbook* to the Bible by Heinrich August Wilhelm Meyer as a fantastic commentary on the scriptures. Also, the *International Critical Commentary* by Driver, Plummer, Briggs; published by T&T Clark of Edinburgh Scotland. Two other commentaries that bring out the Greek beautifully is *Lenski's Commentary on the New Testament* and the *Beacon Bible Commentary*. Also: *Dictionary of New Testament Theology* by Colin Brown.
Dealing with grammar: E.W. Bullinger has an amazing book, *Figures of Speech Used in the Bible* Is a MUST! As a treat, his book *The Witness of the Stars,* every believer must read.

There is a wealth of knowledge contained in the Greek text that is not available in the English language and one of the great joys of this life on earth is to dig for and find those wonderful treasures that God has purposely buried where a devoted student can find them.

I recommend the reader download the computer Bible: e-sword that is found at the website of e-sword.net, which is generously provided for free by Rick Meyers. Download the Bible, then go to the download section of the Bible and find the 1904 Greek New Testament and download that on to your e-sword Bible. This is the text that I used in this book. As you will see there are various translations, dictionaries, commentaries, and a wealth of publications available on the e-sword, as well as a place where you can create your own notes on each verse.

It was in the Navy in 1970, while off the coast of Vietnam that I fell in love with studying the Bible, and this passion gets more intense every decade since. It is my prayer and hope that this book will bless you and inspire you in your love for God's Word.

One more thing, when you read this book, make each page an experience. After you read a verse, re-read it again very slowly and let each word remain on your lips as you pull the full meaning out of each word. Then when you have finished the entire verse, meditate on that verse and open your heart to the Lord, to enlighten your mind to all that is being said. Meditate upon that verse for a little while and In a quiet voice, ask the Holy Spirit to teach you the blazing and brilliant truth behind each verse. This makes reading the Scriptures no longer didactic, but a real-time experience with the Living God.

Εἰρήνη ὑμῖν πᾶσι τοῖς ἐν Χριστῷ Ἰησοῦ· ἀμήν. Ι ΠΕΤΡΟΥ V:xiv

Thomas Moore July 30, 2024, Castle Rock, CO

NOTE: Most Biblical scholars of the 18th, 19th, and 20th century use Roman Numerals for chapter and verse, hence; the student of Scripture needs to become familiar with them. The chapter is in capital numerals, and the verse in small case numerals. This can be confusing as in Luke 7:50, since the small case L looks like this: "l" and can be mistaken as a one, even though a number one is a small case i.

Other books by Thomas Moore from AuthorHouse Publishers.

This book is the result of four years of heavy persecution during the Vietnam war, on a U.S. Navy Ship for being a follower of Jesus, or as my Chief would spit the words in my face: Jesus Freak! I returned love for their hate and completely believed the verse of Scripture that "the Joy of the Lord is your strength" and "count it all joy when you fall into tribulations…" As a result, 10% of the crew give their hearts to the Lord Jesus. During these hard times I sought wisdom and from 1970-1973 I wrote down what the Lord showed me, which is the content of this book: A short story with poems. published in 2004.

Here is the book which is my lifetime achievement. I spent 50 years studying theology and seeking God's Face for wisdom to understand and explain all the intricate details involved with our salvation to show that following Jesus is a love relationship, not a religion. This book intricately explains the closure of the Old Covenant Law by the opening of the New Covenant with the inauguration of the Chief Priesthood of Christ. Also, unique insights into problem Scriptures that have been misunderstood. Very detailed description of the mechanics of Grace and a Holy Spirit led life. It also Includes a massive number of statements from the greatest scholars who ever lived, in almost 500 pages. Published 2019.

This is a small easy to read booklet providing intricate details of all the blasphemies hidden in the common practice of religious tithing that falsely presents Malachi 3:8-11 as a call for Christians to put 10% of their income in the collection plate, as if they are blessed if they do and cursed if they don't. Nonsense! Those filled with the Spirit are led by the Spirit. Also contains massive number of statements from the greatest Bible scholars who ever lived. You will be shocked to learn there is a germ in the religious tithing doctrine that spreads through and corrupts every major truth of the Bible with blasphemy and contains a personal rejection of Christ and a denial of the Gospel. Published 2021.

Special thanks go to Rick Meyers for his e-sword Bible for computer
that is offered absolutely free of charge at www.e-sword.net.

In agreement with our Lord's prayer for you and I:

ἀγίασον αὐτοὺς ἐν τῇ ἀληθείᾳ· ὁ λόγος ὁ σὸς ἀλήθειά ἐστι.
ΙΩΑΝΝΗΝ XVII:xvii

This book is dedicated to the Lord Jesus Christ who
is the Triune God in bodily form, giving Himself
as a ransom for many. Colossians 2:9

Ἐγώ εἰμι ὁ ἄρτος τῆς ζωῆς.

ΙΩΑΝΝΗΝ VI:xlviii

Ἐγώ εἰμι ὁ ποιμὴν ὁ καλός,

ΙΩΑΝΝΗΝ X:xivA

ἐγώ εἰμι τὸ φῶς τοῦ κόσμου·

ΙΩΑΝΝΗΝ VIII:xii

Ὑμεῖς ἐστε τὸ φῶς τοῦ κόσμου.

ΜΑΘΘΑΙΟΝ V:xiv

εἶπε δὲ πρὸς τὴν γυναῖκα· ἡ πίστις σου
σέσωκέ σε· πορεύου εἰς εἰρήνην.

ΛΟΥΚΑΣ VII:1

οὕτω λαμψάτω τὸ φῶς ὑμῶν
ἔμπροσθεν τῶν ἀνθρώπων,...

ΜΑΘΘΑΙΟΝ V:xvi

δόξα ἐν ὑψίστοις Θεῷ καὶ ἐπὶ γῆς
εἰρήνη, ἐν ἀνθρώποις εὐδοκία.

ΛΟΥΚΑΣ II:xiv

καὶ ἡ εἰρήνη τοῦ Θεοῦ βραβευέτω
ἐν ταῖς καρδίαις ὑμῶν

ΚΟΛΟΣΣΑΕΙΣ III:xva

Εἶπεν οὖν πάλιν ὁ Ἰησοῦς, Ἀμὴν ἀμὴν
λέγω ὑμῖν
ὅτι ἐγώ εἰμι ἡ θύρα τῶν προβάτων.

ΙΩΑΝΝΗΝ X:vii

ἐγώ εἰμι ὁ ποιμὴν ὁ καλός, καὶ γινώσκω
τὰ ἐμὰ καὶ γινώσκομαι ὑπὸ τῶν ἐμῶν,

ΙΩΑΝΝΗΝ X:xiv

Ἐγώ εἰμι ὁ ποιμὴν ὁ καλός·
ὁ ποιμὴν ὁ καλὸς
τὴν ψυχὴν αὐτοῦ τίθησιν
ὑπὲρ τῶν προβάτων·

ΙΩΑΝΝΗΝ X:xi

ὁ δὲ εἰσερχόμενος διὰ τῆς θύρας

ποιμήν ἐστι τῶν προβάτων.

ΙΩΑΝΝΗΝ X:ii

ὁ ἀναμάρτητος ὑμῶν πρῶτος
βαλέτω λίθον ἐπ᾽ αὐτῇ.

ΙΩΑΝΝΗΝ VIII:vii

γύναι, ποῦ εἰσιν; οὐδείς σε κατέκρινεν;

ΙΩΑΝΝΗΝ VIII:x

ἡ δὲ εἶπεν· οὐδείς, Κύριε.
εἶπε δὲ ὁ Ἰησοῦς·
οὐδὲ ἐγώ σε κατακρίνω· πορεύου καὶ
ἀπὸ τοῦ νῦν μηκέτι ἁμάρτανε.

ΙΩΑΝΝΗΝ VIII:xi

Ἐν ἀρχῇ ἦν ὁ Λόγος, καὶ ὁ Λόγος ἦν
πρὸς τὸν Θεόν, καὶ Θεὸς ἦν ὁ Λόγος.

ΙΩΑΝΝΗΝ I:i

οὗτος ἦν ἐν ἀρχῇ πρὸς τὸν Θεόν.

ΙΩΑΝΝΗΝ I:ii

πάντα δι᾽ αὐτοῦ ἐγένετο, καὶ χωρὶς
αὐτοῦ ἐγένετο οὐδὲ ἕν ὃ γέγονεν.

ΙΩΑΝΝΗΝ I:iii

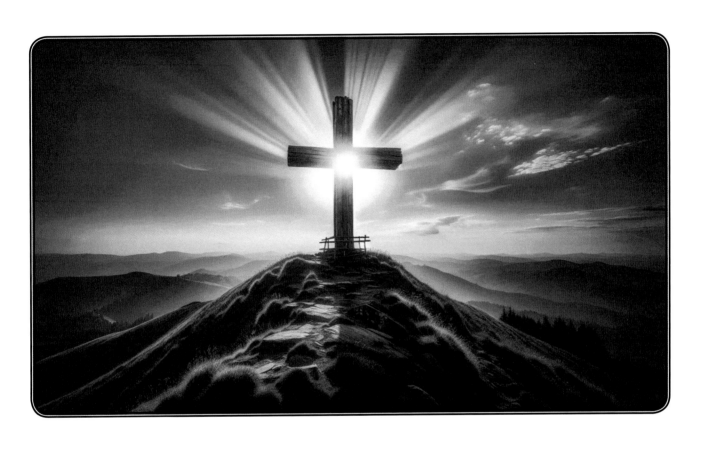

ἐν αὐτῷ ζωὴ ἦν, καὶ ἡ ζωὴ
ἦν τὸ φῶς τῶν ἀνθρώπων·

ΙΩΑΝΝΗΝ I:iv

κἀὶ τὸ φῶς ἐν τῇ σκοτίᾳ φαίνει,
καὶ ἡ σκοτία αὐτὸ οὐ κατέλαβεν.

ΙΩΑΝΝΗΝ I:v

Πάλιν οὖν αὐτοῖς ἐλάλησεν
ὁ Ἰησοῦς λέγων,
Ἐγώ εἰμι τὸ φῶς τοῦ
κόσμου· ὁ ἀκολουθῶν
ἐμοὶ οὐ μὴ περιπατήσῃ ἐν τῇ σκοτίᾳ,
ἀλλ᾽ ἕξει τὸ φῶς τῆς ζωῆς.

ΙΩΑΝΝΗΝ VIII:xii

ὁ γὰρ ἄρτος τοῦ Θεοῦ ἐστιν ὁ καταβαίνων
ἐκ τοῦ οὐρανοῦ καὶ ζωὴν διδοὺς
τῷ κόσμῳ.

ΙΩΑΝΝΗΝ VI:xxxiii

ἐγώ εἰμι ἡ θύρα· δι᾽ ἐμοῦ ἐάν τις
εἰσέλθῃ, σωθήσεται, καὶ εἰσελεύσεται
καὶ ἐξελεύσεται, καὶ νομὴν εὑρήσει.

ΙΩΑΝΝΗΝ X:ix

εἶπεν αὐτοῖς ὁ Ἰησοῦς, Ἐγώ
εἰμι ὁ ἄρτος τῆς ζωῆς·

ὁ ἐρχόμενος πρός ἐμὲ οὐ
μὴ πεινάσῃ, καὶ ὁ

πιστεύων εἰς ἐμὲ οὐ μὴ διψήσει πώποτε.

ΙΩΑΝΝΗΝ VI:xxxv

ὕδωρ ἐπὶ τοὺς πόδας μου οὐκ ἔδωκας· αὕτη δὲ τοῖς δάκρυσιν ἔβρεξέ μου τοὺς πόδας καὶ ταῖς θριξὶ τῆς κεφαλῆς αὐτῆς ἐξέμαξε.

ΛΟΥΚΑΣ VII:xliv

Illustration: hand drawn by our previous neighbor in Warsaw, Missouri.
Ruby Althoff (13 years old) in pencil (one of the most beautiful people you could ever meet).

ὁ γὰρ νόμος τοῦ πνεύματος τῆς ζωῆς
ἐν Χριστῷ Ἰησοῦ ἠλευθέρωσέ με ἀπὸ
τοῦ νόμου τῆς ἁμαρτίας καὶ τοῦ θανάτου.
ΡΩΜΑΙΟΥΣ VIII:ii

εἰ ὁ Θεὸς ὑπὲρ ἡμῶν, τίς καθ᾽ ἡμῶν;

ΡΩΜΑΙΟΥΣ VIII:xxxi

ὃς δ᾽ ἂν πίῃ ἐκ τοῦ ὕδατος
οὗ ἐγὼ δώσω αὐτῷ,
οὐ μὴ διψήσει εἰς τὸν
αἰῶνα, ἀλλὰ τὸ ὕδωρ
ὃ δώσω αὐτῷ γενήσεται ἐν
αὐτῷ πηγὴ ὕδατος
ἀλλομένου εἰς ζωὴν αἰώνιον.
ΙΩΑΝΝΗΝ IV:xiv

εἶπεν αὐτῇ ὁ Ἰησοῦς· ἐγώ εἰμι
ἡ ἀνάστασις καὶ ἡ ζωή.
ὁ πιστεύων εἰς ἐμὲ, κἂν
ἀποθάνῃ, ζήσεται·
καὶ πᾶς ὁ ζῶν καὶ πιστεύων εἰς ἐμὲ
οὐ μὴ ἀποθάνῃ εἰς τὸν αἰῶνα.
πιστεύεις τοῦτο;

ΙΩΑΝΝΗΝ XI:xxv,xxvi

λέγει αὐτῷ ὁ Ἰησοῦς· ἐγώ εἰμι ἡ ὁδὸς
καὶ ἡ ἀλήθεια καὶ ἡ ζωή· οὐδεὶς ἔρχεται
πρὸς τὸν πατέρα εἰ μὴ δι᾽ ἐμοῦ.

ΙΩΑΝΝΗΝ XIV:vi

ταῦτα λελάληκα ὑμῖν ἵνα ἐν
ἐμοὶ εἰρήνην ἔχητε.
ἐν τῷ κόσμῳ θλῖψιν ἔχετε·
ἀλλὰ θαρσεῖτε,
ἐγὼ νενίκηκα τὸν κόσμον.

ΙΩΑΝΝΗΝ XVI:xxxiii

οὕτω γὰρ ἠγάπησεν ὁ Θεὸς τὸν κόσμον,
ὥστε τὸν υἱὸν αὐτοῦ τὸν μονογενῆ
ἔδωκεν, ἵνα πᾶς ὁ πιστεύων εἰς αὐτὸν
μὴ ἀπόληται, ἀλλ᾽ ἔχῃ ζωὴν αἰώνιον.

ΙΩΑΝΝΗΝ III:xvi

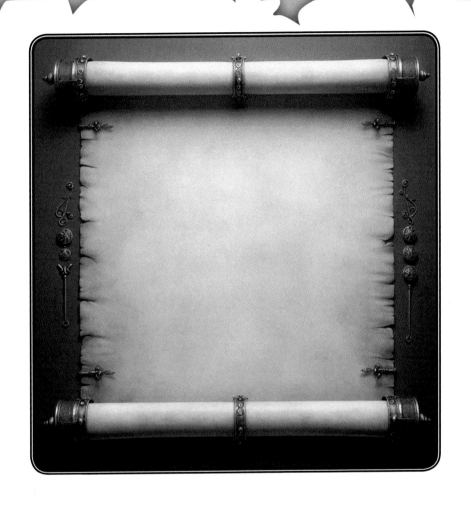

οὐ γὰρ ἀπέστειλεν ὁ Θεὸς τὸν υἱὸν αὐτοῦ
εἰς τὸν κόσμον ἵνα κρίνῃ τὸν κόσμον,
ἀλλ᾽ ἵνα σωθῇ ὁ κόσμος δι᾽ αὐτοῦ.

ΙΩΑΝΝΗΝ III:xvii

ἅγιος, ἅγιος, ἅγιος Κύριος ὁ Θεὸς
ὁ παντοκράτωρ, ὁ ἦν καὶ ὁ ὢν
καὶ ὁ ἐρχόμενος.

ΑΠΟΚΑΛΥΨΙΣ IV:viiib

Printed in the United States
by Baker & Taylor Publisher Services